Sweet Dreams:
Waking Up from a Sleep

Sweet Dreams: Waking Up from a Sleep

ESCAPING THE STIGMA

An Advocacy Story By:

Carmeta Hammond Docherty

To order additional copies of this book, contact:
Xlibris
800-056-3182
www.Xlibrispublishing.co.uk
Orders@Xlibrispublishing.co.uk
769657

Contents

About the Author

Carmeta Hammond Docherty, a vibrant, energetic, and happy soul, is a mother of two. As someone who has a passion for writing, she has always been fond of making novels and writing in script her life story. She loves listening to music, which helps her cope with anything in life. To her, there is always a song fitted for any circumstance happening in her life. Enjoying life in her little abode in Edinburgh, Scotland, Carmeta continues to be living proof that no matter how difficult the paths in life may be, with God, there is always that light at the end of the tunnel.

Introduction

This book is *the story of my life.* It is a story of recovery, a journey of ups and downs, and a declaration of truth. It aims to serve as a testament of how I have been living proof that whatever life throws at you, things still turn out best for the people who make the best out of the way things turn out. Coupled with the stories of the people whom I was with, this book holds the truth that we can do everything through Christ, who strengthens us.

How Advocacy Has Helped Me

I want to talk about the help I was receiving when I was in college and work because I don't want to dwell on the weaker side of me. I want to talk about how it influenced my life and helped me to become a better person.

I first came to independent advocacy because of a mental breakdown following the birth of my two children. Advocacy provides people with a service that helps to open doors and close doors, leading to a pathway of healthy living.

I have stuck with it because if something is good, you don't need to give it up. My life was broken once, and with the help of my faith and advocacy, we repaired it. If it is not broken, you don't need to repair it. Advocacy does not need to be repaired. Good advocacy workers are there as a rock; I lean on them like a shoulder. I didn't expect anything. I just told them how it is. At one point, I was living like a queen because they helped me to get a nanny and a housekeeper. Living in Edinburgh and in a country where people get individual and independent support is where a light can be seen, and I like that. Where else would you want to be?

The second stage was when I was on my feet, because they helped me to get over my weaker side of thinking as well as how I approach life, what I have known, and how I view myself. So I am at a better stage in life for a very long time. As a child, I didn't get a lot of help and support from friends, family, and school. I saw my advocacy worker as an ally who could stand with me when things got tough. My advocacy worker was also my words and voice.

I remember a song when I was growing up and I see my advocacy worker in the words. 'You are the only one that can free yourself from mental slavery, none but ourselves can free our minds.' In that Bob Marley song, I saw the way I use my advocacy worker to lean on and get my voice heard and make things happen. I felt my advocacy worker could move mountains and remove doors for me. So I try not to ask questions. I pray to god, and he puts good people in my life. Having advocacy put people in my life. I don't know if it was faith or not, but I think it is. I thank god I was in a place when things were not good and help was there.

If independent advocacy had not been there, I can't imagine what it would be like. I hope and pray the government can keep organisations like Advocard, CAPS/LEARN, other independent advocacy organisations and Outlook are like a backbone in the city. A backbone supports you and helps you stand. Without that, things collapse.

Having this support helped me stand and gave me more determination. I became a better person. I might have chosen a different path of stigma and more illness than I could cope with. I now think of myself as a light. I would like to know that my life is like a light in the city. I thank god for having advocacy. With my breakdown, it made me feel my life was vulnerable. We all need to play our parts, and advocacy is important. 'No man stands alone, no man is an island, each man brings joy to me, each man's grief is my own.' I like to view that approach to life. That is why I like to share my story of how advocacy has helped me with others. I hope that people will hear about this and want to give their time to help weaker or vulnerable people who face a wall or difficulty. We all have difficulty, whether rich or poor or Christian or non-Christian. Advocacy just gives you the strength to climb that hill.

I hope government can see advocacy as a light in the city. We all have the ability to improve our mental health, and whatever support is there gives people a positive route so people don't need to dwell on other

negative things.

We all have difficulties with mental health, but I didn't

know this. It was good to know I wasn't alone. How

you deal with the difficult things in life determines

who you are. I am pleased that independent advocacy

is a mission that I accomplish with my involvement.

I know life would be impossible without independent

advocacy. I needed to go beyond having a husband

and children. I needed extra support, not just my

family even though it was strong and stable. Family

can sometimes set you back; advocacy can help you

see that the difficulty you are in is not the end. I had

family when I had my breakdown. Having someone

independent made this better. If advocacy had not

been there, my children may have ended up in a home

and my husband might have had a breakdown. Who we ask to help with those ups and downs makes a difference.

I am realising my dream of writing a book, and all this is like in a dream waking up. Somehow it's a dream that is coming to reality, and I am glad I have the opportunity of giving my story to others. I hope they can see that being young as a woman and having children is not the end of the world, as long as you see your life is a story that can help change peoples' lives and help them find direction. Don't be afraid to ask for help. Just know who you are asking. It all plays a part. I am also launching my T-shirt designs. I hope that people take inspiration form the designs in my T-shirts, one of which says, 'As an orange gives vitamin, so as Christ gives everything and to me he has no rival or equal.' Likewise, independent advocacy

like CAPS and Advocard, as well as Outlook, have no

rival. They give everything to me. Why not you?

A wise man has power, but a man of knowledge

increases strength. Please consider independent

advocacy, because it can give you strength. And

get to know about it. It is a service worth knowing.

Thank you.

How Adult Education Has Shaped My Life

After losing myself to mental illness and being unable to provide for my children, I found myself in a halt— in a halt to do something. To do anything. To do everything that I have been doing and all the things that I have been wanting to do. And that I need to do. I was in a void where it seemed like nothing could be done.

Eventually, I found myself being engaged in adult education. Through it, I gained understanding about my illness. And for me, this is very important. If you understand what you are and what you are going through, it gives you more understanding of what to do and what needs to be done so that you can continue to live. Continue to do what you need to do, and do what you want to do.

Adult education is wonderful. It's beneficial. It's helpful. It keeps your mind off your illness. The focus is on group discussions and learning activities instead of the illness being the focus of the group. And because of that, it gives you rest. Because of that, you can think away from your illness. Because of that, you can make a much more positive framework in life.

The Interviews

The interviews are feedback from people who travelled with me along the path towards my advocacy. Touching lives and changing futures along the way.

Interview 1

New Skills – finding pride within yourself and learning how to rise up after adversity.

Interview 2

Time Will Tell – good time spent with good company and allowing time to sink and let it do the healing.

Interview 3

Mirror –opportunity to reflect and ponder upon your current stage and introspect for change and development

Interview 4

Confidence –skill and talent acquisition for self-worth and self-efficacy towards team improvement.

Interview 5

Collaboration –people with self-worth and vision working together towards development and recovery.

Interview 6

Adults Education –focus on individual differences and how to use them to one's and the community's advantage.

Interview 7

Shake –provide opportunities for yourself and others.

Interview 8

Young People –the children are the future. Nurture and educate them of what is right and help them shape a brighter future for all.

Interview 1 New skills =finding pride

Interview 2 (by the writer of the book) Mirror = causes Changes

Interview 3 Talents he gain =confidence

Interview 4 Close at hand.

Interview 5 Support virity of class =Education

Interview 6 Different people with confidence.

Interview 7 Adults Education = Photographer teams focus not on self etc weakness of character .

Interview 9 give yourself a shake = talks

Interview 10 (by the writer of the book) Young people

= need supporting

Interview 11 Time will tell =good time

Part 2

To the unknown of how where life will take them

so what influence your mind is what you becomes.

So HealthPower. Is down to wisdom of your mind.

Mind teachers us and how you views your mentel state

of mind that give us our character and =give us our

personalities = ie Behaviopur

Favouris is when we develop wisdom and stature and

in favour with God and humans. I personally feel

when you are in favour of mental state of mind you

can conquer =any force in your health or ones mind.

So be careful of and whose influence you.

Find favour with yourself. So I can say find favour

with yourself. So I can say as one as favour in self and

mind. Great Bob Marley he said this. Free yourself

from mental slavery none but yourself can free yourself

mind.I personallythink the types of people who you

are around for longer time spam can changes you and

palaces you goes. can definitely be the tools and the

trade of the types of skills of experience can be the out

come of how you think about mental health problems.

Also causes you to thinks of a free mind also nothing

can weaken your mind else you will never free from

mental illness. Which is becoming a serious threat to

tomorrowsworld..

Interview 6 See differences in people's

People in the the world that see my views. May Christ

Grant His Favour and shines His light on us.

Any thing you are doing do it with a passion.

Have a passion

Win wirh a passion

Play with a passion

Stand with a passion stand against with a passion.

Part 3

The Author learning centre they are supportive they

never give up on me even when I gave up on myself of

becoming an Author. I know I will be out there still

thinking of how I can becoming an Author. It will

be something I think off and not a reality. Now its in

words and able to read. also will be able to share to

many countries.

Part 4

Golden rules I experience in life.

Learn before you are older

Read while you can reading and listening to others.

In your development and been older and talented as an Author.

Help others while you can

Owner felt if you are wrong.

Each other's graves is my own.

Each other's joy shiuld be joy to others

leaning not on your own understanding

Read while you can

Visit a cinema as much as you can

Encourage others as offen as you can in something good

All ways be happy to choose not to be a victim all ways ready to speak out.

Always ready to escaping the stigma that life can puts in your path way.

Stigma can be the mind which is fracture and capture the mind causes to view one in the wrong way. of others, which can be ture as a mirror with dubble sides.

You can watch and view my interview here: This is the interview link. https://vimeo.com209132815

Thankyou

Search for the Unknown

'I think. Therefore I am.' As the famous niche goes, what we think and what we instill in our minds is definitely what we become. Power of the mind is perhaps the strongest force there is. That is why it is always best to nurture your mind. Educate yourself. Continuously. Learning is not limited to years in school rather it is a life-long process. Mental Health is something that we must prioritize in our daily living. Because the condition of our mind will be the condition of our body and the state of our soul. It dictates our personality. It hones our attitude.

With this, one must always be careful of what we let into our minds. Be careful of who we deal with. Be mindful of who we interact with because influence is something that might affect our state of mind and something that could alter our well-being.

Altered mental state is something that is threatening our future. It is something that is in the verge of haunting our future and our children's future. Therefore, all of us must work towards better mental health. All of us must join hands and work for a better future. The Kingdom of God is for those who think well. And do well. Let us aim for a well living so we may live a well life.

Be the master of your own mind. Just like what *Bob Marley* once said, *'Free your mind from mental slavery. Let no one but yourself control your own mind.'*

My Journey as an Author

Who would have thought that I would end up becoming an author? Never in my wildest dreams did I think that one day I would be writing and publishing something that could help a lot of people. Not just myself but also people from other regions and other countries in the world.

This journey, I owe a lot to the community which has helped me accomplish all these things. The *Author Learning Center*. A supportive community where I met a lot of people that helped me develop my talent in writing.

To end, let me leave you, my readers this…

Have a passion.

Work with passion.

Live with passion.

Win with passion.

Escaping the Stigma

I feel I haven't elaborate on my book name. I thankyou I have the chance to do so reader's let I say this .Beause I personally think stigma is a better photo of one individual self.stigma is in eveyone of us either way. Negative or positive its is an opinions about others. Most of the time is the negative comments about others. Thats makes or form a character of the person that felt stigmatized.Its up to the individual how they becomes a victim of that bolly. or a victim in the past or present.

personally I think if I Wasn't sure ones mind can deturn one health. thats how am able to be stronger. on my views on mental health then it would be different. If it wasn't my culture myself and my up bringing I would be an oppressor. x an intimidator x. Because I am a victim from childhood plays a part of my mental health after the birth of my children. I know you can't afford to be focusing on mentality ways of life.

living in a culture that mental illness or anyform of stress can give you a label that can change your character for good or even your life. If you are a younger mother then your chances of getting a career is over.

Now they are saying young children and younger people are having mental health.

I feel that they are getting too sencnti about one state of mind. I know for sure at that age group most of the time these children and younger people needed good mothers and fathers or even a guardian to be there and needed encouragement. Mothers needed to be supported when having children. for at least till their child or children. reached the age of 5 what is most important Outlook should and can be available to be there for every mothers and father's with mental health or without mental illness. Children need more stayable home good mothers and father either one or both parent company 24 /7

Britain don't need doctors that will influence parents thats their children or having mental health problems without given them proper support in there pregnancy. Society are influence by professionals and professional services and they can get it wrong and most of the time. I feel how you think about your self-esteem can changes you ,and your homes.Your home also can transform their actions also your children and younger teens. I felt as a mother with a health problems such as breaks downs. my children were in good form for now because I did not pass on my health problems such as breaks over thinking. my stress to them. I felt as a mother I never stops been a mother. a child needs to know that. by living in a stable condition that needed a home needed such as no alcohol. no illegal drugs. Drugs alcoho theses issues is one main source of marriage or family home to birth negative thinking and weak thoughts poor judgment of character and the a reason why your children to be prioritised no drugs no alcohol in your home then you are opening doors for doctors to label your child or children with mental health. Because my experience is as a child mental health is up to your up bringing your sourond your environment state of mind. and your culture and people and your city plays a big part in your life. as a child mental health is not something you think about a good self-esteem is up to your company. The encouragement you receive. The manner in which your parents spoken to you. Children needed to good influence to knows that they are the best thing in life.In a good county like Britain Ifelt that the passion to be the best is not a priority. like my country in Jamaica every children singing Jamaica land we love sining Jamaican are the best. For my children they missed out on that about Britain. As soon as my children reached knowledgeable age they don't have that drive in knowing they are in a great country. they wasn't aware of Britain and that they can become someone who can grow up to be greater man or woman. or no awareness of this is a great country. and everyone wanting to be here no matter what they do or where there from they just want to be British citizens. rich or poor. So British children need a bit more backbones knowing there are one of the best in the world.

I know this country did not help me not to developed mental illness problems But it helped me to cope with my health problems such as breaks downs stress. i felt if this culture was more like the culture I was brought up in. then I wouldn't be with out a labels and with so much labels and professional services to tell you. You are unwell with mental illness its becoming a serious threat to parents and if you wanting your children to get a good start in life.

where so much professional services for people who wants to makes money by tell you that your child or children are having mental health problems. Because the government will support theory that you need to abels your child so that they can be professional and become rich. am not against been rich but against telling me am noone and label is best suited young children.

Shaking off Mental Health

People that creates stigma and stress can not see there ego. Because in there head they are superior. while others quality are poor. they say they are creative while others are not useful. They say they are never wrong. also they say we needed them. Yet we are confused to them.

People that are overcoming mental health issues most of the times there are the ones seems to have the upper eage of things. 1 They are like sponge they observer like tongue with a taste of not putting up with a

weakness in life such as mental illness they are the
one that speak less listen more.

while others are interested in seeing your tears they
don't listen they do less, work less.

I dont think of myself been number one but I think
others should always be ready to be prepared to climb
any mountain gose up any ladders and battle any
battles. also

Encourage yourselves and believe in God and his
Son. My closer friends said about me they say I am
stronger.

My weaker side I have listen to others that thinks
mental health problems can have the number one place
in your life or even something you can't overcome in
life.

For a long time I see that way But I pulled myself together and say

No to mental stress such as No to alcohol. No to drugs.

No to to others that will make me think mental issues is my companion and away of normal life.

Everyone who's reading our story and views from the Outlook team to mental illness. Everyone are prone to some sort of mental illness is how we approach matters in our life and the stigma we accept the Xphysically of your mind.

(2) Theses are some phylogenetic mind set l like doing to help me to cope with anything in life with my personalities, Xfactors

I dont do always as I pleases I aways prepare to do as
God say.

I don't worry for too long.

I listen to others more than usal

I learn new skills when I can

Always ready to pray. always praying.

Life is good when you satisfied with something small.
or a small gift

I believe in hope.

Hope is gone for others when they have high
expectations of the wrong way or wrong things.
Wrong God

we should not only fight for Blood Tears Sweat and
Love Only.

But for the Fare of God to be seen able around the
world.

Without the fare of God we are always in need

With the fare of God there is no want.

I once as a post card said

Good friends are like STARS,they come and

go but the ones that stay are the ones that GLOWS.

Friends like these we are not a Lone

So I Thank God.

(3) Always prepare to surprise others:

Always ready to speak out always ready to go that

extra mile.

Always wanting to be ready to do more.

Always be there for others as offen as you can.

Never do:

Dont ready to be the miss goode goode when things

not good when others been bad.(why bean a hypocrite)

These do and don't dose help me on my journey of

bean the person of who I am today. these are like pills

to the pain

Joy to the sorrows .

No one wanting mental health but no one is above

mental illness

Your culture

Your life

Your Idols

Your God

Your friend's

Your drives

Your pressure in life Your passion you have

these are the things that's helped me, and can help you

overcoming mental health issues.

Some people don't want to be well while some wanting

a life free of stress there are no such thing thing as

no stress

While others prolonging stress in others life. there are

the oppressor.. who is the oppressor your mind.

Thank you for reading.

My readers

I want to let you in a secret about myself. Which thats makes me who I am today

I always thinks of how most peoples thinks of me. In my head I believe this Carmeta.

Oh she is a Dragon puffins fire and fiery. But I consider myself a good friend of the lion.

So having the Air and fields to explore with nothing to fear.

This Dragon knows the power of the dragon and God.

I believe I just have to go around the Conner to change.

I consider myself a survivor of the battle of air and

fields and above is the only place I want to be.

I want to meet my friends and family there.

This is my father's world and heaven

He will be giving me one monument in time. I just

want to make that differences with it when he dose

in this life or next.

These are words that in courages I

I have a dreams and a songs to song to help me cope

with anything.

I says a prayer with no one in sight. but I know he is

there.

My heart willl goses on

on and on

So thankyou. from Carmeta Hammond Docherty

Saying to you believe in yourself and God and his son.